Poet in the Kitchen

Poet in the Kitchen by Moira Andrew & Jenny Ranson

Published by Poetry Space Ltd 2021

Recipes: Jenny Ranson

All recipes are for an approximate number of servings

Cover artwork: Jane Burn
Colour Illustrations: Jane Burn
Black and white illustrations: Susan Jane Sims

Acknowledgements

Some poems in this collection have been previously published by Indigo Dreams Publishing

Scone recipes are derived from those in the Glasgow Cookery book

Lemon Posset recipe from *Rhodes around Britain,* BBC Books, 1994

Poetry Space Ltd Company Number 7144469

Reg.Office 2 North St, Beaminster, Dorset DT8 3DZ

Printed and bound in Great Britain by Whitehall Printing Co. Ltd

www.poetryspace.co.uk

ISBN: 978-1-909404-43-4

Poet in the Kitchen

by

Moira Andrew & Jenny Ranson

Moira Andrew was born and educated in Scotland. She worked as a primary school teacher, and a college lecturer in Scotland, a head teacher in Bristol before becoming a freelance writer in Wales where she lived with her second husband Allen. She has written poetry for children, and educational publications for children and teachers, and has toured schools encouraging children to write poetry. After her husband Allen died in 2003 Moira moved to Cornwall. Nowadays she lives with Norman in Nunney, Somerset and focuses on writing poetry for adults. She has three recent collections: *Geese and Daughters*, (IDP), *Looking Through Water*, (Poetry Space Ltd) and *Imagine a Kiss* (Dempsey & Windle). Until recently, Moira and Norman spent several months a year in Cyprus.

Jenny Ranson is Moira Andrew's daughter. She is a talented cook who first gained an HND in Catering & Hotel-keeping in Aberdeen. After a serious illness, she converted her qualification to a Diploma in Dietetics. She worked for several years as a dietician for the NHS. She lives in Cornwall and now teaches swimming part-time. Jenny is an enthusiastic gardener and has developed a beautiful flower garden which follows the seasons. She is currently working on an allotment where she grows her own vegetables. She is an accomplished baker - loves baking bread, cakes and other goodies for friends and family.

Moira Andrew

Jenny Ranson

For Fiona and Ian

for Norman

and in memory of Allen

Contents

Poems

Recipes

KITCHEN DRAWER

Not for kitchen cutlery the luxury
of plush-lined pockets, regimented
wedding-present canteens – they come
as a hotch-potch of oddments, mixed race,
uncertain backgrounds, remainders, survivors.

They're placed in wire trays
in some kind of order, teaspoons,
vegetable knives together, blades
facing away, but what about rarely-used
things, like the pizza-cutter, kept *just in case?*

I tip them out, spoons and knives, forks,
whisks, tin-opener, bottle opener, skewers.
I clean the drawer with a kitchen wet-wipe, dry it
with a paper towel, wash the mismatched cutlery.
They all have their stories these left-overs –

Grandmother's spurtle, a wooden stick, unused,
 (I don't like porridge),
her child-sized rolling pin, a favourite utensil,
 (makes my daughter smile),
a silver teaspoon marked DNB,
 (my mother's newly-wed initials),
a new potato peeler.
 (the old one has lost its bite),
a champagne cork,
 (from our 10th anniversary)

Knives and spoons from other people's kitchens –
two tiny coffee-bean spoons,
 (the other lost to my ex-husband),
the only tablespoon,
 (bequeathed by my mother)
a large silver fork of unknown ancestry,
five refugee dessert-spoons
 (from my husband's ex-wife's widower?)

Job done, I replace the clean cutlery,
spoon by spoon, fork by fork,
a new-fangled plastic net
for unscrewing reluctant tops
cheek by jowl with bone-handled left-overs-
scissors, bread-knife and wooden spoons
easily accessible at the front –
and push the drawer closed.

HONEY CAKE WITH SPICE

Honey is the ideal breakfast spread – especially with new bread and butter. It is also delicious in a cake flavoured with spice. (Delia Smith's idea, although I have altered her original recipe).

Ingredients
For the cake:

75g clear runny honey
225g self-raising flour
1 teaspoon ground ginger
1 teaspoon cinnamon
75g brown sugar
Grated zest of one lemon
110g butter
1 egg

For the icing:
175g icing sugar
1 tablespoon lemon juice
Preserved ginger

Cuts into approximately 8 slices

Method

Pre-heat the oven to 180C. Butter and lightly flour an 18cm cake tin. Weigh out 75g of honey by first weighing a small basin then adding the honey to the correct amount. Warm the honey in its basin in a pan of simmering water. Sift the flour and spices into a large bowl, then add the sugar and lemon zest. Mix. Cut the butter into small pieces and rub into the flour until it looks like breadcrumbs. Mix in the beaten egg and warm honey. Beat well with a few teaspoons of water, if required. Spoon the mixture into the prepared tin and spread evenly. Bake for around 50 minutes and turn out on to a wire tray to cool. When cold, coat with the icing sugar mixed with lemon juice, adding a thimbleful of warm water if necessary.

Decorate with preserved ginger pieces cut small.

HONEY FOR BREAKFAST

It's supposed to be good
for you, *Start the day*
with a proper breakfast,
     they say.

Toast, crisp buttery toast,
honey from a round bellied
pot, snug in the hand as
     a Cox's pippin.

Unscrew the lid, a smell
of summer, dig into dark
thick sweetness, spread
     like varnish.

Bite, leave toothmarks,
savour the flowery golden
taste, *unique* it says on
     the label.

Read on. *To collect this*
jar of honey, it is estimated
that bees travel two orbits
     of the earth.

Then, *They visit up to*
a million flowers. A million?
Our table is dizzy with the
     buzzing of bees.

BREAKFAST WITH SWALLOWS

Black wizards on the wing
skiing the slopes of air
landing with precision
on the washing line
voices replete with song
they pause, titivate, nibbling
at pale under feathers
one careful wing at a time
remember the partner
on the nest, visit briefly
bearing a beakful
of thread-fine insects.

They pirouette, showing off
their skills as trapeze artists
completely ignoring us
sitting in the morning sun
a striped umbrella shading
the bowl of fresh fruit
our coffee and toast.
We chat in the fractured
fashion of familiarity. Above us
the birds chatter too, an
ongoing repetitive conversation
each sequence ending
in the same purring trill.

I imagine they feel safe
comfortable in their skins
(as do we) allowing us
to share their music
their yellow mountain air.

GOING SOLO
(Swallows mate for life)

He haunts
the telephone wire,
assiduous, patient
perched neatly
as a crotchet
on a song sheet.

He opens his beak
and sings, voice
robust as ever
filling the evening air
with hope, with
a terrible sadness.

Each call ends
in the same
tremulous trill,
loneliness
in every last
piercing note.

He gives stray
females the push
as he waits
for his one-and-only
singing his songs
of incredible longing.

EASTER BREAD

She limps up the hill,
basket on her arm,
offers us a traditional
Easter treat.

She could have
come from some ancient
painting, headscarf, apron,
long patterned skirt.

Flaouna, she mutters
handing us a miniature loaf.
We mumble our thanks
fumbling in unfamiliar Greek.

But the gesture is
world-wide, a gift, one
from an impoverished
old woman living alone.

The bread, we learn
is made from flour, sugar
and herbs galore. It's plaited,
looks quite beautiful.

At lunchtime, we share
the little loaf – *Interesting,*
we agree, practising
thank-you's in our best Greek.

Efharisto poli, Marina!

BREAKFAST IN COLOUR

A great start to the day – in colour! And so simple. The poem 'Breakfast with Swallows' pictures Norman and me having breakfast under a sun umbrella on the upstairs patio in our house in Cyprus, swallows constantly on the move, busy nest-building and feeding. Imagine our sadness when on our next visit the following spring, the male swallow was on his own. As it says, in 'Going solo', he sang his heart out to no avail. Breakfast on the patio just wasn't the same.

Ingredients

1 ripe Galia melon
Bunch of green seedless grapes
Bunch of black seedless grapes

Serves 4

Method

De-stalk the grapes and drop into a bowl. Cut the melon in half, then each half into four. Remove the pips and cut half the melon into bite-size chunks. Put directly into a wide-mouthed serving bowl. Add half the grapes, cut in half and sprinkled over the melon chunks. Then repeat for the rest of the fruit. Cover and place in the fridge overnight. A juicy and colourful breakfast treat.

LIVING THE DAY

Cracked ice of morning,
birds unzipping the day,
     dreams in flight.

Craving coffee, black
and strong, toast, a shower's
     pinpricks on skin.

Ghost footsteps die away,
routine takes over, mug
     plates rinsed clean.

The cat, surrogate mate,
deigns to lap-sit, yawns, spruces
     up her image.

What now? Diary dates
diminish. Only photographs
     tell it as it was.

Max out the hours, fill to
overflowing with silent words,
     e-mails, poems.

Make soup, chopping onions
into diamonds, ribboning
     carrots and leeks.

Cut a closed camellia bud,
watch its petals unfold, making
     love to the sun.

Listen to blackbirds spinning
songs among the leaves,
     time dawdles.

At last, the sky bronzes, cat
purrs, birds quieten, ghosts
     unbutton their coats.

FRUIT FOR BREAKFAST

It's a bowl I use every day,
shallow, in white and blue,
patterned round the edge
a sea-creature on the base
its out-of-kilter fishy eye
          leering up at me.

I stand at the kitchen window
slicing melon into bite-sized
chunks, add cut-up grapes,
green and black, to the mix
to store in the fridge for
          tomorrow's breakfast.

He comes up behind me, steals
a bit of melon. *That bowl,* he says,
*we bought it in Singapore, one
of two, it was – until I broke one.
I've always liked it.* A casual
comment. So much I don't know
about this man.

So much he has to learn about me.

LEEK AND POTATO SOUP

An easy soup to prepare, one that the men in my life have enjoyed eating. I think it is the sheer abundance of potato that appeals to them. As Allen, my husband, used to say, 'A meal isn't a proper meal without a helping of potatoes!'

Ingredients

25g butter
1 large onion
3-4 medium leeks
4 (or more) large potatoes
seasoning
2 stock cubes made up with 1 litre water
Fresh or dried parsley
A glass of white wine (not essential)

Serves 4 - 6

Method

Melt butter slowly in a large saucepan. Peel and finely cut the onion. Fry gently in the butter. Wash and chop the leeks, discarding the outer leaves. Add chopped leeks to the pan. Simmer for five minutes until soft. Add wine (if using) and made-up stock. Peel and chop potatoes into chunks. Season well. Add the potatoes into the pan. Bring to the boil, then turn down to a gentle simmer. Simmer for 20-25 minutes until potatoes are soft. Sprinkle with parsley and serve in bowls with chunks of fresh crusty bread.

LENTIL SOUP

Of course, they were young
and there was the baby, crying
chuckling crazy 24-hour baby –
And the well-worn clothes (except
for the child's) and living
with hand-me down furniture all
boxed together in a single room.

29th April, her birthday, barely
a bus fare between them, end –
of -the- month lentil soup time
and he brought home a box,
a ribbon-capped shining box
and a bunch of anemones
for the baby to give.

The baby wanted to eat them
so they traded flowers for
rusks and still the box, like
Pandora's, unopened in her hands.
'Go on,' he said. White lace
foamed and bubbled across green
candlewick, not of their choosing.

But how?' 'The office sweep,'
he said. 'The National – I put
a quid on the beast and it won!'
The baby drummed heels on her chair.
They fed her bread and soup as
white frills spilled, by chance,
over sooty-eyed anemones.

LENTIL SOUP

As it says in the poem, lentil soup was an end-of-the-month staple when we had a young family and very little money coming in. The recipe that follows is simply an outline – the joy of lentil soup is that you can explore the vegetable basket and use whatever you find there! It's a very accommodating soup.

Ingredients

1 onion
Knob of butter (about 25g) or a slick of olive oil
Carrots
Tomatoes (even squashy ones!)
Parsnip (not essential)
Leeks (not essential)
2 medium potatoes
1 tin of chopped tomatoes
2 stock cubes made up to 1 litre
Glassful of white/pink/red wine (again a delicious addition, but not essential)
Handful of red lentils
Water to soak the lentils
Seasoning
Dried parsley

Serves 4 –6

Method

Soak the red lentils in boiling water. Melt butter in a large saucepan. Add chopped onion and leek (if using). Add the made-up stock cubes and wine. Simmer until soft. Add peeled and chopped vegetables - carrots, tomatoes, potatoes and/or parsnip (or whatever you've found in the vegetable basket!). Simmer for a few minutes. Add the contents of a tin of tomatoes and water to cover. Bring to the boil. Sieve the soaked lentils and add. Season. Simmer for 20-25 minutes. Blend, a few ladlefuls at a time. Top with flaked dried parsley and serve with chunks of bread.

CHEF'S SECRET

No kitchen whites, no frenzy,
no serving bell, just a man
in a red sweatshirt, white hair
shower-neat, a thin thread
of cigarette smoke needling
the busy morning street.
Oscar lay at his feet.

We traded small-talk. Then
I tried to prise a recipe
from him. His tomato soup
was out of this world, thick,
rich, Chianti-red. 'No secret,'
he said. 'You need tomatoes,
tomatoes and more tomatoes.'

'But there must be more to it
than that,' I persisted. The dog
stirred, looking up. Andre's
soft Italian burr became
more pronounced. 'Just use
enoff tomatoes,' he said.
'I'll sort out a recipe next time.'

There was no next time.
The bell was stilled, kitchen
clamour silenced. The chef's
secret was safe. But he lives on.
When I make soup, I hear
simmering echoes of his voice,
'Just use *enoff* tomatoes.'

TOMATO SOUP

Andre's tomato soup was out of this world and prising a recipe from this busy chef was almost impossible. All he would admit to was using 'enoff' tomatoes. So, to make a rich soup use as many tomato left-overs as you can find lurking in the fridge.

Ingredients

Large onion
25 g butter
Around 800g tomatoes peeled and chopped to make *'enoff'*
1 large or 2 small tins of chopped tomatoes
Juice of one orange
Glass of white or rose wine (optional)
500-600 mls chicken stock homemade, ready made or from stock cubes
Fresh or dried parsley

Makes 4 generous portions

Method

Using a large pan, slow- fry the onion in the butter. Add the fresh and tinned tomatoes and simmer until soft – about 5 to 10 minutes. Add in the stock, orange juice, parsley and wine, if using. Bring to the boil and simmer for about 15 minutes. Sieve, liquidise or use a food processor.

Serve with a little more parsley and a swirl of cream

COCKALEEKIE

Like Auchtermuchtie
it's difficult for Sassenachs
to get their tongues around it.

On a dreich winter's night
at my grandmother's table
it's the perfect comfort food.

And so easy, onions and leeks
sautéed in butter, pearl barley,
stock, parsley and pepper.

Grandfather, napkin tucked
over navy waistcoat, clasps
the soup bowl in both hands.

He blows, tests, relishes
each spoonful, wipes white whiskers
with care, holds up an empty plate.

Any more in that pot of yours?

COCKALEEKIE SOUP

A firm Scottish favourite, easy to make and very tasty. Allen, my Welsh husband loved it. It's a soup well-remembered from childhood, made in both my Mum's and my Gran's kitchens. (Although neither included wine in the recipe!)

Ingredients

25g butter
1 large onion, chopped
3 leeks washed and chopped
850 mls chicken stock (homemade, ready-made or made up from stock cubes)
A glass of wine optional
100 g pearl barley
Dried or fresh parsley
Freshly ground pepper

Makes 4 generous portions

Method

Put the barley in a bowl and cover with boiling water. Leave to soak for 5-10 minutes. Melt butter in a large pan. Add the peeled chopped onion and leeks, with the parsley and pepper. Cook on a low heat until soft, (about 5 minutes). Pour the chicken stock over the onions, leeks and wine, if using. Bring to the boil. Drain water from the barley, then add barley to the soup. Simmer for about 20 minutes until barley is well cooked. Taste and season with more pepper if needed. Serve with chunks of crusty bread

SCOTCH BROTH

There's a ritual to its making.
First, chicken bones simmer
in a crock-pot, kitchen filling
with the heady smell and
      rich steam.

Once strained, stock glistens
and thickens in a jug, waiting
its turn. Pearl barley soaks in
hot water and butter splutters
      in the pan.

Onions, shorn of their paper
skins, go under the knife and
fall as diamonds. Leeks make
green and white ribbons on the
      chopping board.

The pointed toes of carrots
are cut into streamers, diced.
swedes fight every step of the
way, reluctant to give up their
      winter coats.

Finally, they too, fall victim
to the blade, adding their yellow
stars to the mix, a mosaic of
jewelled vegetables, sizzling in
      melted butter.

Stock, seasoning, a flutter
of herbs and the soup bubbles
on the hob. Just one hour later,
a rainbow of flavours tantalises
      the tastebuds.

CHILDHOOD TREAT

My grandmother's panacea
for every ill, (and none)
white sugar and yellow butter
on white crusty bread,
(not quite the thing for a dentist's
daughter, but I don't think Dad
ever found out.) Tens of years later,
off my food, stomach gurgling
and twisting, I don't fancy soup, not
even my homemade leek-and-potato,
my fallback, banana-toast is out too,
no banana. In the bread-bin, a new loaf,
fresh from Sainsbury's. The smell
reminds me of that childhood treat.
I cut a thick slice, lash on butter, shake
deep layers of white sugar on top,
leave satisfying tooth-marks
in the butter. I still feel guilty, but
Gran's secret remedy hits the spot.

ST LEONARD'S PUDDING

Well, bread and sugar, an undoubted treat in Gran's estimation – was an answer to every child's problem as far as she was concerned. When I buy a fresh loaf, often still warm, my treat is to spread a slice liberally with butter and top it with golden syrup. It too, brings back memories of my lovely grandmother. But it's hardly worth a recipe! So here is another childhood favourite. It has been made (and still is) by three generations of our family. A comforting pudding for a cold winter's day.

Ingredients

2 tablespoons red jam (strawberry, for preference)
40g plain flour
40g butter
275ml milk
2 eggs, separated
2 dessertspoons caster sugar for the filling
75g caster sugar for the meringue

6 servings

Method

Spread the jam over the bottom of an oven-safe pie dish. In a saucepan, melt the butter gently. Mix in the flour, stirring well, and cook gently for a few minutes, (allowing the flour to cook). Remove from the heat and stir in the milk, a little at a time beating well between each addition. (You might need a balloon whisk for this). Place saucepan back on to a low heat until gently bubbling. Do not overheat. You will see the sauce beginning to thicken. Beat all the time, (again you might need the balloon whisk). Take off the heat and beat in the egg yolks one at a time, then stir in sugar. Cool slightly and pour the custard mixture over the jam. Cool in the fridge.

Make the meringue topping by whisking the egg whites until just stiff. Then fold in the caster sugar. Spread the meringue over the cooled custard mixture and cook in a preheated oven at 130C for about 15-20 minutes, until golden brown. Reduce by 20C for fan ovens.

CROSS-PURPOSES

I meant to give you
     a flower
clove-pink for perfume,
perhaps a penstemon
     for colour.

I lost the words,
     offered you
a stone instead. It lay
uncompromising, heavy
     in my hand.

You misunderstood, broke it
     like bread,
Its yeasty smell filling
the room, crumbs falling
     at my feet.

In return, you gave me
     a handkerchief
too fine for tears. I
expect you intended a rose
     long-stemmed.

QUICK BROWN BREAD

Now if there was ever a smell created to alert the taste-buds, warm bread, fresh from the oven, fits the bill. With lashings of butter and perhaps a helping of honey, lemon curd, jam or golden syrup, newly-baked bread is a treat hard to beat.

Ingredients

5oog mixed strong white and wholemeal flours

25g butter or vegetable fat

7g instant dried yeast

1 ½ teaspoons salt

1 ½ teaspoons caster sugar

300mls hand hot warm water

8 thick slices

Method

Mix the flour salt and sugar. Rub the fat into the flour.
Mix in the salt, sugar and dried yeast. Add the water and mix to an elastic dough.
Knead well for about 10 minutes.
Divide between 2 small or 1 large well greased loaf tins.
Cover dough with oiled polythene. Put in a warm place and prove for at least an hour till well risen.
Uncover and bake for 25-30 minutes at gas mark 7/220 C. Reduce by 20C for fan ovens.
Bread is cooked when you can hear a hollow sound when tapping the base.

LEMON CURD

Absolutely delicious with fresh bread and lots of butter at breakfast time. We always find that lemon curd made in Cyprus with lemons fresh from the tree is even more delicious than that made at home with shop-bought lemons. But that may be because of the ambience, cooking in a kitchen overlooking the village of Kalo Chorio with its red-tiled roofs, church spire and the blue hills beyond. The view itself makes you want to spend time preparing food, even a slow recipe like lemon curd. Bread and butter spread with sharp lemon curd straight from the fridge is a great start to the day – especially for breakfast on the terrace in Cyprus.

Ingredients

4 medium lemons
110g butter
275-350g caster sugar
4 eggs, lightly beaten

Makes about 2 jars

Method

Grate the lemon rind into a basin, then add the squeezed lemon juice. Cut the butter into smallish chunks and add to the juice along with the sugar. Place the basin over a pan of simmering water and heat gently until the butter melts. Slowly add the lightly beaten eggs stirring all the time until the mixture thickens and coats the back of the spoon. (Patience required for this step - but it's worth it!) Do not over cook or let the mixture too hot. Pour into warmed jars. Cool, cover and store in the fridge.

ALL NIGHT PARTY

Late nights have never been my thing,
so I've no idea how I coped, dozed
on the boyfriend's shoulder I expect
to brighten up in the small hours.

We listened to records, to the boyfriend's
party-piece, *Honeysuckle rose,* played
with speed and flair. We jived, smooched,
snogged, changed partners, drank wine.

One of the boys grilled bacon for baps.
I remember the sizzle, the smell, that first
salty bite. I remember a girl sitting at the
top of the stairs, the sound of her crying.

Behind drawn curtains, the group fractured
into pairs, less laughter, more fumbling.
I remember the door opening to birdsong,
to the liquid light of a summer morning.

BACON BAPS

Just writing the words bacon baps brings that special salty smell, making my mouth water. They are the ideal party snack – especially as the clock moves towards 2am and people are beginning to yawn, thinking of looking for coats and car keys. But the smell of your host rustling up bacon changes all that. Bacon baps, served hot just dipped in fat, outdo every takeaway known to man!

Ingredients

8 soft bread rolls
A slick of oil
16 rashers of streaky bacon

Serves 8

Method

In a heavy frying pan, heat a little oil. Fry the rashers over a medium heat for 4-5 minutes. (Turn halfway through cooking). Open the rolls, dip briefly in the hot oil. Insert two crisp rashers in each bread roll. Slice in half and serve on hot plates with a glass of wine or beer – or a mug of hot black coffee. Magnificent party food!

(The trouble is that your guests will now be reluctant to leave the party!)

FEEDING SALLY'S HENS

Kate and I stand
on the wall and our
plastic bags rustle.

Sally's hens, fat as
feather dusters on legs,
jostle and bustle.

They scurry, dust
flurrying where they've
scraped the earth bare.

We throw bread. They
scrum down, brown
trousers up in the air.

They run at us, beady-
eyed ladies with skinny
pink-stockinged legs.

We laugh. They burble
like bubbles in bottles,
smell as warm as their eggs.

They peck and push,
bargain-hunters braving
the school jumble sale.

We leave them noisily
squabbling over cabbage
and stale curly kale.

SPICED PORK CHOP WITH APPLE SAUCE

Makes a delicious evening meal – excellent in the apple season when the trees are loaded with fruit.

Ingredients

Pork chops
Mixed spice
Oil
seasoning

For the apple sauce:
2-3 firm apples
25g sugar
Ginger wine (with water) or ginger beer

Allow 1 - 2 chops per person

Method

Pour a little oil into a heavy frying pan and heat. Pat the chops dry and spread a thick coating of spice over both sides. Season. Fry quickly on both sides, then turn down the heat. Continue to fry until the meat is cooked.

Meantime, peel and slice the apples. Cook in a pan with sugar and ginger beer or watered ginger wine until soft. (around 10 minutes). Mash the apples with a fork. Keep hot. Pile on top of the spiced pork chops. Serve with boiled potatoes and minted peas.

SATURDAY LUNCH

We'd finished our meal
when the call came – mince
and potatoes. I remember.
My then-husband, strangely
quiet, had pushed his plate away.

The children took this as
a signal. *Please can we get
down?* I muttered to myself
as I scraped leftovers
into the bin.

I thought of the
time I'd spent, chopping onions
browning meat, peeling potatoes,
I don't know why I bother.

My husband walked the floor,
window to window, window
to window. *What's the matter?
Ants in your pants?*

*Don't know
don't feel right. Think I'll
nip down to 'West of
Scotland', watch the game,
maybe meet the boys*
I was glad to see him go.

The phone rang. I downed the
tea- towel. Milngavie 7691…
silence at the end of the line,
a clearing of the throat, *The thing is,
John's dead.* All the air
drained out of the room. My
husband's brother…and somehow
he knew, he knew.

COTTAGE PIE

It took a long time before I made cottage pie again after the tragic telephone call from the Isle of Arran. (See 'Saturday lunch'). However, I can remember my grandmother producing a beautifully browned cottage pie from her old white-enamelled gas oven in her kitchen, carrying it steaming hot into the dining room where Grandpa was waiting, white napkin tucked under his chin. He liked to serve out the pie while Gran served the accompanying vegetables, usually carrots or mashed swede, freshly dug from the back garden.

Ingredients

25g oil
1 onion
450g lean minced beef
Salt & freshly milled black pepper
1 level tablespoon plain flour
Small tin tomato puree (65g)
300 mls stock
1 glassful red wine (optional)

For the topping:
700g potatoes
Seasoning
A little warm milk
25g butter
Chopped parsley

4 servings

Method

Heat the oil in a large saucepan. Peel and slice the onion and fry gently to soften, (for around 5 minutes). Then add the minced beef and seasoning. Fry the meat until it is browned. Sprinkle the flour over the meat and add the tomato puree, stock and wine (if using).
Cover and simmer gently for ½ - 1 hour, checking from time to time that the mixture isn't sticking to the pan. Add a little water if required to slacken. Allow to cool, then transfer to a pie dish. Heat the oven to 190C. Reduced by 20C for fan ovens.

Meanwhile peel and cut up potatoes. Cover with cold water and bring to the boil. Cook until potatoes are soft. Then drain and mash thoroughly. Add seasoning, milk and ½ the butter. Spoon the potato topping over the meat and spread evenly. Dot the surface of the potato with the remaining butter. Cook in the oven for about 30 minutes until bubbling and brown. Sprinkle with parsley before serving. Serve with root vegetables , carrot, parsnip or mashed swede.

CHILD WITH A CAUSE

My grandmother was chicken-plump.
She wore long earrings, smelled of
Pears' soap and lavender water.
She kept cream in a jug under
a blue-beaded net.

Grandfather kept us both
on a tight rein, our place
at the kitchen sink. When Gran's mind
slipped slightly out of gear
I was her memory.

Nearly always, that is. She peeled
potatoes once, put them ready
for Grandfather's tea and forgot
to light the gas. He was furious.
I saw Gran's tears.

Upstairs, in the narrow hall
I waited, scuffing the turkey-red rug.
He took his time. The flush thundered.
His shape vultured against
the door. I was raw

as carrion. *It's not fair.*
You made Gran cry. He lunged at me.
How dare you, child? How dare you
speak to me like that? Picked clean
by anger I ran.

Don't mind him, my grandmother said.
He likes his tea on time. The matter
was closed. Grandfather tore into
his beef stew, dumplings and gravy.
I pushed my plate away.

BEEF GOULASH WITH DUMPLINGS

My grandfather, with his white whiskers, deep voice and piercing blue eyes, could be quite formidable to a child – and indeed to my grandmother. Thinking back, I was a very brave child to stand up to him as I did. It took me a long time after the 'Child with a Cause' incident to enjoy beef stew (or goulash) with dumplings once again.

Ingredients

4 tablespoons olive oil
700g (approx.) braising steak
1 tablespoon plain flour
2 teaspoons paprika
2 onions, thickly sliced
2 garlic cloves (crushed)
Beef stock (either home-made or from stock cubes)
75ml red wine
2 tablespoons tomato puree
2-3 peppers of different colours
Salt & pepper
Water
A handful of frozen peas

Serves 4 — 6

Method

Heat the oil in a heavy pan. Add onions and fry for 5 minutes or until soft. Meanwhile, mix the flour with paprika, add seasoning and coat the chunks of steak. Remove the onions to a bowl and brown the steak in the oil. Stir all the time as the floured steak will stick to the pan. Add the cooked onions, red wine and stock. Reduce the heat to simmer. Stir in tomato puree. Prepare the peppers by de-seeding and slicing. After 30 minutes add the peppers. Keep a jug of water on the side of the cooker, adding a little water at a time to slacken – every 15 minutes or so. Simmer for 60 minutes or until the beef is tenderised. Add frozen peas.

For the dumplings:

110g self-raising flour
55g Shredded suet
Water—enough to make a soft dough, not too wet
Salt & pepper

Method

Mix the flour, seasoning and suet in a large clean bowl. Gradually add the water. Flour a board and with floured hands, roll the dumpling mixture into 10-12 balls. Re-heat the goulash mixture, spoon into a heavy oven dish. Place the dumplings on top and cook in a hot oven, (220C for 20 minutes. Do not use the lid – the dish should be open. Check that the dumplings are beginning to brown. Serve hot – with or without another vegetable.

APPLES

Apples look like Christmas baubles
    hanging from a tree.
They smell just like a summer breeze
    tickling the summer sea.

Apples feel smooth as china cups
    on display inside a case.
Shaken, they sound like a baby's toy,
    rattling in front of his face.

But the taste of an apple is best of all,
    first biting through the skin,
when the fruit is crisp and crunchy
    and the juice runs down your chin.

BAKED APPLES

Ideal for late September when the apples trees are laden down with fruit. The fillings can be altered and/or added to – it is a very accommodating recipe. Delicious served with cream, custard or ice-cream.

Ingredients

One medium/large crisp apple per person.
To serve four:
4 apples
4 dessertspoons muscovado sugar (1 for each)
2 teaspoons cinnamon
4 dessertspoons sultanas or raisins
Knob of butter for each apple, (about 25g)
2 tablespoons water – or even better, ginger beer

Method

Set the oven to 180C. Wash the apples. Run the tip of your knife around the middle. Then core the apples and place in a baking dish or tin. Mix the sugar, butter and cinnamon, then fill the well in each apple with the mixture. Measure the water or ginger beer and pour into the dish round the prepared apples. Bake at 180C for about 30-40 minutes. The apples should look fluffy and soft. The water (or ginger beer) along with the sugar and butter will have made a delicious syrup in the baking dish. Serve hot from the oven with custard, cream or ice-cream.

Try chopped dates, chopped apricots and/or almonds as an alternative filling.

FORBIDDEN FRUIT

The woman stands naked
but for a scarlet sunhat.
She wriggles her toes
in the warm earth, stretches
sun-baked arms, sighs.

A fine-tuned breeze fingers
the fruit trees, tickles
their brittle leaves, sun
touching up the orchard
with hot searching hands.

The man can't believe
his luck. He loiters in
the shadows, watching,
waiting. The woman reaches
for a low-hanging branch.

Breasts taut, nipples proud
she selects an apple, twists
it from its twig. She cups
its weight in her hand, pulls
down the brim of her hat.

She sits, takes a first bite.
The man makes his move,
steps into the sunlight, folds
the woman in his arms, kisses
her, tasting the sweet juice.

Forgotten, the apple falls
to the ground. *It's true,*
the man thinks, *Red hat, no
knickers*. A worm squirms
from the apple's white core.

APPLE CAKE

A lovely sweet for the apple season. In our Somerset garden we have two apple trees, laden with fruit from late August onwards. It takes all a cook's imagination to come up with new ways to use the apples before the birds demand their share of the autumn treasure. The apples, green on one tree, red on the other, look beautiful as they hang from each branch like coloured lanterns.

Ingredients

225g self-raising flour
2 teasp. ground cinnamon
115g unsalted butter, chilled and diced, + extra for greasing
115g brown sugar
1 large egg
8 tablesp. milk
225g Granny Smith, Bramley or other hard apples, peeled and sliced
100g sultanas
2 tablesp. Demerara sugar

8 slices

Method

Turn the oven to 180C, gas 4. Reduce by 20C for fan ovens. Grease and line a deep 20cm with baking parchment.

Mix flour and cinnamon. Add diced butter and rub into the flour until it looks like breadcrumbs. Stir in sugar. Add the beaten egg, followed by 6-8 tablesp. milk – the mixture should resemble a thick smooth batter.

Add the apples and sultanas. Mix. Scrape the batter into the prepared tin and level it. Sprinkle with the Demerara sugar.

Bake for 30-40 minutes until golden brown. Test with a skewer in the middle until it comes out clean.

Allow to cool for 15 minutes and then turn out on to a wire rack.

GRANDPA'S TREASURE CHEST

He examines each one
with intimate care
rolling it round
in his big earthy hands
picking prying poking
like a monkey
searching her baby for fleas
selecting only perfect specimens
polishing each smiling face
with a clean cloth
wrapping it in a twist
of greaseproof paper
and placing it
in an old dressing table drawer.

I try to help, *This one Grandpa*
I say scooping up
a hard greeny-brown apple
its skin rough lustreless
Can you no see, child?
he says pointing out a tiny wormhole
Go and badger your Gran
she hovering in the kitchen doorway
waiting for him to explode
in exasperation – his Russets
are an annual labour of love
needing total concentration,

huffing and puffing
his white moustache
wet with spittle
Grandpa ranks the last apple-parcels
tight as Terracotta warriors.
Gran and I barely breathe
as he performs a last rite
covering the drawer
with gently tucked-in newspapers
before bearing the whole thing.
up to the attic
in ceremonial procession
Gran steadying the steps
me drinking in the nutty bittersweet smell.

MY MOTHER'S CRUNCHY APPLE PUDDING

Still a family favourite, especially on a cold autumn day. My frugal Scottish mum used to make this pudding regularly – it uses up dry bread and makes a wonderful crunchy topping. A pudding for the apple season – and beyond.

Ingredients:

3 or 4 hard green apples (Granny Smith for preference)
75g caster sugar
½ teacup water (ginger beer or ginger ale) approx. 140mls

Topping

175g breadcrumbs (made from dry bread whizzed in a blender)
75g shredded suet
75g brown sugar
Teaspoon ground cinnamon
25g butter

6 servings

Method

Peel and slice apples. Simmer in a pan with water (or ginger beer), enough to just cover the apples. Add sugar and cook until beginning to soften. Meantime make the topping by combining the breadcrumbs, sugar, shredded suet and cinnamon. Spoon the cooked apples into an oven-proof dish and top with the dry ingredients. Press down. Dot the topping with butter and place in a pre-heated oven (180C Cook pudding for around 25 minutes or until topping looks brown and crunchy). Serve with cream or ice-cream. Delicious!

AUNT JEAN'S SUNDAY LUNCH

Lockdown, no fresh fruit -
we're delighted to find
a tin of Libby's peaches at
the back of a cupboard.
The smell, the slimy juice,
and I'm back at Aunt Jean's
for our once-a-month visit,
done up in our Sunday best.

Sisters, Aunts May and
Jean, lived in a gloomy
upstairs flat with Miffy,
an enormous smelly cat.
So different, Aunt May,
a thin austere woman,
Aunt Jean plump, outgoing.
with thick bandaged legs.

Lunch, a white starched
tablecloth, heavy silver
cutlery, a casserole of some
kind, overcooked vegetables
And always, as a special treat,
tinned peaches with tinned
cream. My daughter smiled
grimly, feigned enthusiasm.

A lockdown tradition, the
6 o'clock phone call, to
exchange the day's trivia,
a wasps nest in Jenny's shed.
My news is less dramatic,
finding a can of peaches,
a reminder of Aunts Jean
and May and Miffiy, the cat.
*So that's why I hate tinned
peaches!* my daughter says
I've always wondered.
Bye, speak again tomorrow.

A NICE CUP OF TEA

They tell me
I make a good cup of tea –
not that I'd know
I don't drink the stuff,
can't stand the smell,
astringent, sour, thoroughly
unappetising.

I've brewed tea
first thing in the morning
for the men in my life –
and for my daughter,
a compulsive tea-Jenny
(well-named) She takes it
milky, by the bucketful.

I remember making tea
for my mother, bringing it
to her bedside, she in curlers
and blue hairnet. She struggled
to sit up, *Thanks dear*, she said,
not knowing. I had to tell her,
Mum … Dad died in the night.

CHRISTMAS TRADITION

I know it's popular, especially
around Christmas, but there's
no way I'd try anything going
by the name of *Sherry Trifle*.
It's bound to be a let-down,
a complete sham, thin red jelly
and peaches in packet custard
with precious little sherry.

My grandmother didn't drink,
of course, no self-respecting
grandmother did in those days.
But when it came to making
the traditional Christmas trifle,
that wasn't a problem. Her
version was second-to-none, rich,
the very smell intoxicating.

A ritual business, it was, the
oval crystal dish taken down
from a top shelf and washed
in warm soapy water and one
by one, the ingredients assembled,
thick jam, dark with strawberries,
eggs and milk, a black vanilla pod
like a tiny wrinkled stocking.

The dish was crammed with
sugar-crusted, jam coated sponge
cake. Then came the ceremony
of the sherry, measured into a blue-
rimmed egg cup. One cupful, two –
she lost count – and upended the bottle.
'Must be thoroughly moistened,' she said,
sucking sherry-soaked fingertips.

The whole thing was topped
with egg custard and whipped cream
forked over into a swirly feather
pattern. It was put in the larder
to cool. Compared with today's pale
imitations, there's no contest. To
make proper *Sherry Trifle*, you need
sherry, lots of it – and no counting.

GRAN'S SHERRY TRIFLE

Christmas would not be Christmas in our house without Gran's sherry trifle served in its special oval dish. My grandmother rarely drank anything alcoholic, just a small glass of sherry on special occasions, so she had no idea of how much sherry to use in her trifle. She simply kept on pouring it over the sponge, a glassful at a time, until it was soaked with sherry – it was always fiercely alcoholic and quite delicious.

Ingredients

A pack of trifle sponges (or even better, home-made sponge cake)
A jar of (full fruit) strawberry jam
3-4 sherry glasses of sweet sherry (or to taste)
Custard:
> **250g butter**
> **250g caster sugar**
> **250g flour**
> **2 eggs**
> **Approximately 300mls full-cream milk**
> **Vanilla essence**

Double or whipping cream

Serves 8

Method

Smear the trifle dish with strawberry jam. Don't stint – make it quite thick. Cut the trifle sponges into quarters and spread thickly with jam. Pack the sponges tightly into the dish. Now pour the sherry over the sponge pieces. Mash gently with a fork. (This is where my Gran went to town. She used lots of sherry). Make sure the sponge is well soaked. Top with any spare jam. Leave in the fridge for about 15 minutes while you concentrate on the custard. Make a roux with the butter and flour. Stir in lightly-beaten eggs. Add sugar and a few drops of vanilla. On a low heat, carefully add milk a little at a time. Keep stirring the mixture until it thickens. Pour over the sponge and jam trifle base. When cooled, leave overnight in the fridge. Top with whipped cream before serving.

CHRISTMAS

Carol-singing in the frosty air.
Holly wreaths all down the stair,
Reindeer galloping across the night
Ivy looped with tinsel bright
Stockings hung on ends of beds
Trees dressed up in golds and reds
Mince pies ready, spicy and hot,
A baby in a manger cot,
Stars to guide kings all the way
…….And we wake up to Christmas Day.

TRADITIONAL MINCE PIES

I have a confession to make – I'm not very keen on mince pies, but I know that they are an essential Christmas treat for many people.

Ingredients –for 12—16 pies

Mincemeat filling

450g Bramley apples (peeled and chopped small)
225g shredded suet
800g mixed fruit (raisins, sultanas & currants)
225g mixed candied peel
350g dark sugar
Grated zest and juice of 2 oranges
Grated zest and juice of 2 lemons
4 teaspoons mixed spice
1 teaspoon cinnamon
4-5 tablespoons of brandy

Milk to coat
Icing sugar for sprinkling

For the pastry

350g plain flour
75g lard
75g butter
Pinch salt
Cold water to mix

Oven temperature 200C

For the filling: Combine all the ingredients except the brandy in a large mixing bowl. Stir thoroughly, cover and leave for 24 hours. Place mixed ingredients into a pan and simmer for 30 minutes. Cool and add the brandy.

Make up the pastry by sifting the dry ingredients in a mixing bowl. Rub the fats into the flour until it looks like breadcrumbs. Add just enough cold water to mix to a dough that leaves the bowl clean. Wrap the dough in cling film and leave to rest in the fridge for 20 minutes or so. (Or de-frost a pack of frozen pastry and use this!)

Grease the patty pans. Roll half the pastry, cut into rounds and line the tins. Fill these with mincemeat. Dampen the edges and cover with the rest of the rolled-out pastry. Make a hole in each mince pie and brush with milk. Bake for 25 minutes or until golden. Sprinkle with icing sugar and cool on a wire tray.

FRUITCAKE

we stand together
on the back step
out of sight
licking spice from our fingers

Even better than your mother's
Dad says
But don't let on –
she'll never forgive me

not a cake at all
sultanas, brown sugar, currants
baked in crisp pastry
(Mum's speciality)

I've pinched her recipe
added cinnamon, apples
a hefty sprinkling of ginger
Just up my street, Dad says

Mum tuts
You were sent to try me!
her skills lie in the kitchen
mine in words, in paint

and here I am
beating her at her own
game
I can't blame her
for having a go at me

co-conspirators
Dad and me
brushing away
telltale crumbs

FRUITCAKE

Fruitcake, made by the following method – more fruit tart than cake! – was my mother's speciality. It would never have done to let on that my dad enjoyed my efforts even more than hers. After all, she was the cook in our family! So Dad and I hid together, out of Mum's sight, eating our slices of my fruitcake with its extra cinnamon and spice, pretending to chat about the weather or golf or the grandchildren – anything other than my fruitcake-baking skills. Hence the poem.

Ingredients

7 inch oven-proof plate

200g shortcrust pastry
350-450g– fruit – apples (ideally Bramley apples), currants and sultanas
75-100g brown sugar
1 teaspoon mixed spice
½ teaspoon ground ginger
1 ½ teaspoon cinnamon
1 teaspoon cornflour
2 tablespoons water (or ginger beer)

8 slices

Method

Set oven to 220C, reducing to 180C after 10-15 minutes cooking

For the filling:

Peel and chop the apple and mix with the sugar, currants, sultanas and spices. Heat in a large saucepan with water (or ginger beer) to soften the fruit. Mix the cornflour with a little water and add to the fruit mix to thicken slightly –allow to cook for a few minutes then remove from the heat. Cool.

Divide the pastry in two. Roll out the smaller part to fit the plate. Use this section as the base. Put the cooled fruit mix onto the pastry. Spread out just short of the edges. Wet the edge of the pastry lining on the plate. Roll out the remainder of the pastry slightly larger than the plate and place on top. Press the edges well together and mark with fingers or a fork. Make a small slit on top to let steam escape while cooking. Brush with milk.

Bake using the middle of the oven. It is useful to put the prepared tart onto a tray before putting in the oven in case of any fruit leakage,

Cook for 10 minutes at 220C. Reduce by 20C for fan ovens. Then cool to 180C/160C, cook for a further 15 minutes or until golden brown. Remove from the oven and sprinkle with caster sugar while still hot.

DAY OUT WITH GRANDPA

There's some noisy man-talk
from the yard, a snare-drum
sound of boots. Pigeons hang
in squalid bundles, head-down
like broken guns. The spigot
spouts water over bare brown
backs and dangling braces.
Grandpa, in Harris tweeds,
leans on a stick, every inch
Laird of the Manor.

The kitchen is low and dim.
Marigolds in jars blaze on
the sill, the open door a
cube of sunlight. *Ready
Mother?* the men call. Shy,
I slide into the shadows
till they find their places
round the table. Grandpa
sits at the head, says grace
into sudden quiet.

Mrs Campbell is hairpin-thin.
She lifts a man-sized griddle
from the stove, heaps steaming
oatcakes on to plates. As they
eat, the brothers rumble on,
butter running unnoticed
down thick fingers. Grandpa
delicately wipes his white
moustache. I juggle oatcakes
too hot to handle.

Time to go. Grandpa thanks
Mrs Campbell, fumbles for change.
The brothers look up, *See you, Sir,*
they say. We walk in single file
down the lane. Grandpa with
his gun and two pigeons, dead
as dreams, swinging in a bag.
The bus takes us back to town,
to the day-job, Grandpa shrinks
in front of my eyes .

OATCAKES

An outing with my Grandpa – a highly unusual event. I remember how he play-acted his lord-of-the-manor character over the Campbell boys and how utterly embarrassed I was in consequence. Mrs Campbell's fresh oatcakes were fantastic, but I remember restricting my appetite in an attempt not to appear too greedy.

Ingredients

225g medium or fine oatmeal

15g melted vegetable fat or butter

1 level teaspoon salt

Good pinch bicarbonate of soda

Hot water to mix

Makes 8

Method

Add salt and bicarbonate of soda to the oatmeal. Pour in the melted fat.

Mix in enough hot water to give a workable consistency.

Knead to form a dough. Divide into 2. Make each one into a round .

Roll each round quite thinly and cut into 4 triangles.

Sprinkle a little oatmeal on top.

Cook on a hot griddle or flat bottomed frying pan .

When cooked on one side, - 3-4 minutes- put onto a tray and into a cool oven to dry off. Or under a medium grill but watch carefully.

Enjoy with butter and maybe honey!

COCOA AND CRUMPETS

Fuelled by adrenaline
after a successful gig
you can't sleep, yawn, turn,
toss. Sex doesn't work.
We are mesmerised by
the shipping forecast,
shift back to back. Sleep
remains a world away.

Give up? you say, flicking
on the bedside light. We
pull on dressing gowns,
stumble into the kitchen,
pop crumpets in the toaster.
Butter melts, puddles
yellow over white plates
I make cocoa, you Horlicks.

We talk, hold hands,
unpick the gig. *I forgot*
to sing the last verse of
Careless Love, you say,
Did you notice? I didn't.
Posh candle-lit suppers
are all very well – sometimes
hot crumpets hit the spot.

SCOTCH PANCAKES

Yes, crumpets are OK, but they can't hold a candle to Scotch pancakes! (Or drop scones as they as also known).

Pancakes/Drop Scones

Ingredients

225g plain flour
1 ½ teaspoons baking powder
½ teaspoon salt
1 tablespoon caster sugar
1 large egg
275 ml milk (approx)

Makes 12 –14

Method

Mix the flour, baking powder and salt.

Make a well in the centre, add the egg and about half the milk. Mix to a smooth batter.

Gradually beat in the rest of the milk to make a thick batter. You may not need all the milk.

Drop the batter in spoonfuls –tablespoon is a good size – on to a hot greased griddle or flat bottomed frying pan.

Cook the pancakes for about 2 minutes until the top begins to bubble. Turn and cook for a further 2 minutes on the other side. Cool in a tea towel on cooling tray.

Eat with butter and jam.

CRACKERJACK

I loathe porridge
always have.
They used to sit me
in front of the mirror, trying
to spoon the gloop
into my mouth,
The baby in the mirror
will eat it up …
as far as I was concerned
the baby in the mirror
was welcome to it.
I was about 18
when, out of the blue,
my mother said
You really don't like porridge,
dear, do you?
Yet give me fingers of Crackerjack
(pure porridge oats)
now sticky and sweet
and I'll down them
by the plateful.
Had Crackerjack
been on offer,
that baby in the mirror
would've been
first in the queue.

GRAN'S CRACKERJACK

Another family favourite. I can see my mum, in a yellow-checked apron, in our small kitchenette with the back door open, mixing porridge oats into the butter and syrup with a fierce intensity. For those few moments, nothing else was of any importance, neither the sound of a telephone ringing in the hall, nor the insistent 'When will the Crackerjack be ready?' questions from impatient children.

Ingredients

225g rolled oats
170g butter
140g caster sugar
Pinch salt
1 good tablespoon syrup

Makes about 14 slices

Method

Melt the butter and sugar in a pan. Add the syrup and melt gently. Mix the porridge oats and salt in well to melted mixture. Pour into a greased baking tray (30x20cm). Push well into corners.
Bake 15-20 minutes at gas 5/190C
Score into squares, allow to cool before transferring onto cooling tray.
Store in an airtight tin.

PARTY PIECE

My husband was no cook,
his preferred environment
an office desk, pens
and pencils neatly aligned,
in-tray stacked with files,
each numbered, named,
dates strung on green tags.

As far as he was concerned
a meal wasn't a meal
without potatoes on the side,
baked, roasted, mashed.
From time to time, if I wasn't
around, he'd venture into
kitchen territory to boil a pan
of potatoes, timer in hand.

But he had one party piece
recipe handed down from
mother to son. He'd commandeer
the frying pan, whisk and mix
in secret communion. Tea-towel
over one shoulder, he'd magic up
a tray of spiced Welsh cakes –

not exactly Masterchef, but
pretty damn good for a non-cook.

WELSH CAKES

As it says in the poem, my husband was no cook. To be fair, he had looked after himself for several years when he lived on his own, but his skills didn't go much beyond cold meats and boiled potatoes for every meal – potatoes were an essential! Baking was not in his skill-set, but his Welsh cakes, from his mother's recipe, were fabulous – Allen's piece de resistance. Here is his recipe, found in my daughter's recipe book with notes in his careful accountant's handwriting.

Ingredients

225g self raising flour
Good pinch salt
1 teaspoon mixed spice
100g butter or margarine (or mix half butter and half vegetable fat)
60g - 75g caster sugar depending how sweet you like them
75g currants and sultanas mixed
1 egg beaten
Good teaspoon golden syrup

Makes 12—14

Method

Mix the flour, salt and mixed spice then rub in the fat until you have a consistency of breadcrumbs.
Add the sugar and dried fruit.
Pour in the beaten egg and syrup and mix to a stiff dough. Use your hand if easier.
Roll the dough to about 5mm thick and cut out into rounds with a cutter.
Bake on a hot griddle or flat bottomed frying pan until golden brown on both sides. The cakes should still be a little soft in the middle.
Dust with caster sugar. If there are any left can be stored in an airtight container or freeze.

CINNAMON PASTRIES

A green-panelled kitchen, deep white sink,
gas cooker, sunshine falling in neat squares
across the floor. My grandmother, in flowery
wrap-round apron and crystal-drop earrings,
      mistress of the rolling pin.

I stand on tiptoe, watching and waiting. Face
rosy with effort, Gran beats butter and sugar,
flour and eggs into a gooey mix. She adds
cinnamon, the colour of brick-dust, powdery,
      spooned from a doll-sized jar.

She stretches the pastry, rolling it one way and
another, turning and knocking it into a neat block
on the marble slab. Cut into rounds, dusted with sugar
and it's ready for the oven. A blast of heat
      as she opens the door.

A spicy smell rises, dancing in the motes
of sunlight filtering through the window. I hover
at her elbow. *Go on,* she says, *Outside!*
Help Grandpa tie up his sweet-peas. I'll call
      you when they're ready.

Ten minutes and the pastries are lifted,
hot from the oven, crisp and brown and sugary,
their alchemy complete. Gran's recipe
whose proportions only she knew, is lost, but
      still, the rich smell lingers.

CINNAMON BISCUITS

Cinnamon pastries from my grandmother's sunshine kitchen – I can still smell them cooking, their spicy sugary smell, all these years later. Gran's recipe was lost long ago, but we have found a similar one for cinnamon biscuits (see below) - although they don't quite match the pastries of my memory – maybe nothing ever will.

Ingredients

225g self raising flour
¼ teaspoon salt
½ level teaspoon baking powder
100g butter
110g caster sugar
60g currants or sultanas
2 teaspoons cinnamon
I medium size egg
2 tablespoons milk

Makes about 14

Method

Sieve together the flour, salt, baking powder and cinnamon. Rub the butter into the flour mixture. Stir in the sugar. Beat the egg and milk together and add it to the mixture. Mix to a stiff dough. Roll out on a floured surface to about 1/2 to 1 cm thick Cut into rounds. Put onto a greased baking sheet, well spaced out. Prick with a fork.
Bake in a preheated oven for 15—20 minutes at gas 5 or 190C Allow to cool for a few minutes.
Sprinkle a little caster sugar over the top before completely cool Then lift onto wire tray to finish cooling.

GREEN MAGIC

Wake up one morning and
it's wall-to-wall green - *Green?*
As in bottle, malachite, jade,
only the yellowing edge of cloud,
the grey of sky, a backdrop.

Overnight? Absolutely true -
from bone-bare branches to the
blowsy richness of spring,
the plain-and-purl of fields,
the unravelling of birdsong.

Impossible! Look - green
as far as the eye can see,
grass luminescent in first light,
layer upon layer of leaves
softening every tree-shape.

You on speed or something?
No need, simply open a
window, breathe the early air
and give free rein to colour,
as in lime, chartreuse, viridian.

You mean green?
Yes, green.

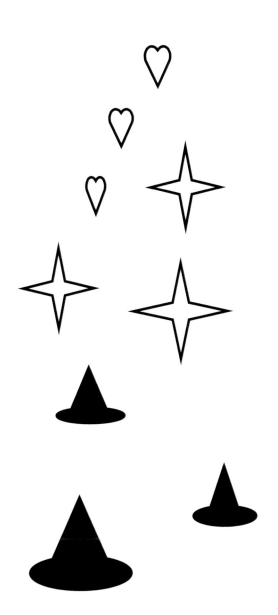

MAGIC

Maybe it's something
to do with that magic number
the stuff of fairy tales
      three sisters
            three kings
                three wishes
laid out on the worktop
the ingredients
don't look anything special
      a bag of flour
            caster sugar
                a box of eggs
weighed out
the magic three
weaves its spell
      3 oz flour
            3oz sugar
                and of course 3 eggs
but whip eggs and sugar
to the gold
of Rumpelstiltskin's hair
      and fold in flour
            then into the oven
                where the alchemy of heat
does its thing
conjuring up a sponge-cake
      light as air
            nectar-sweet
                but beware

it comes with a bad-fairy curse….

TRUE SPONGE

To maintain the magic of this recipe, we have used ounces. True sponge is like the three wishes of fairy stories, it takes three of everything – eggs, flour, sugar, butter. Magic indeed!

Ingredients

3 medium eggs
3 oz plain flour (75g)
3 oz caster sugar (75g)
3 oz melted butter (75g)
½ teaspoon baking powder
3 drops vanilla essence

For the filling

Small carton double cream 2-3 tablespoons jam, preferably raspberry or blackcurrant

Cuts into 8 slices

Method

Preheat the oven to 180C. In a large mixing bowl beat the eggs and sugar until thick and creamy. (You should be able to leave a trail from the whisk in the mixture). Melt the butter gently in a sauce-pan. Do not allow to bubble. Allow to cool slightly. Add ½ the flour with the baking powder, then ½ the melted butter to the egg and sugar mixture by carefully folding in. Now add the rest of the flour and melted butter, again folding in with care. Keep as much air in the mixture as you can. Pour the mixture into a well-greased 18cm round cake tin. Bake for 30-40 minutes until firm and golden brown. Cool on a wire tray.

When cool, split the cake and spread the jam over the bottom half and top with the beaten cream. Sprinkle the top with caster sugar. Cut and eat as soon as you can. Enjoy this 'magic' cake!

STOLEN GOODS

In this land of lemons
she is one fruit short.
Easter. Every shop is shut.
Don't fuss, he says
I'll get you another one.
They grow like weeds here.

And he's off down the lane.
Minutes later, he hands her
a plump juicy specimen
complete with leaf and stalk.
Where? she asks. *I stole it*
he says, with a thief's grin.

She rasps fine nubbled skin
on the grater, squeezes juice
folds sugar and beaten eggs
into the mix, adds cold butter
cut into bite-sized pieces
as in her daughter's recipe.

She stirs the fragrant mixture
over simmering water
willing it to thicken, pots up
into three warm jars
of jewel-bright curd ready
for tomorrow's breakfast

Spread thick on toast
it tastes sharp and tangy
yellow as the morning sun.
Cook and thief smile
in complicity, the stolen
lemon giving that extra zing.

JENNY'S LEMON POSSETT

If my daughter Jenny is invited out for a meal in a friend's home, she will usually ask if there's anything they'd like her to bring along. With one voice they request Jenny's lemon posset! It's my favourite dessert too!

Ingredients

600ml double cream
155– 170g caster sugar (depending how sweet you like it)
Juice of 3 large or 4 small lemons

Makes about 4 small portions

Method

Boil double cream and sugar for 3 minutes. Make sure you use a strong flat bottom pan.

Take off the heat and pour the lemon juice into the cream and sugar stirring briskly as you pour, ideally using a balloon whisk.

Cool slightly then pour into ramekin dishes or glasses.

Allow to set in the fridge 2-3 hours.

Serve with fresh raspberries and maybe some shortbread. Or just pour over a little cream.

GEESE AND DAUGHTERS

It's preferable to raise geese than daughters
(Chinese proverb)

Geese? They strut
around the farmyard
sleek off-white
peering down
on their world from
haughty rooftop eyes.

Daughters? They kiss
you good-night from
wet pink mouths, dance
in your arms to jazz
on the radio, stamp
in red-cheeked fury.

They grow up, phone
to tell you stuff,
make sure you're OK,
bake scones for you,
buy you flowers
for the kitchen table.

Give me daughters
any time. No doubt
geese are all very well
in their way, but
only those few who
lay golden eggs

MISS LENNIE'S SODA SCONES

Miss Lennie was my daughter's favourite teacher – what Miss Lennie said was gospel. She taught cookery at which Jenny excelled – even regularly winning first prize in her year. Soda scones are a favourite in our family, especially when Jenny arrives to make them. Try the scones hot from the pan with butter melting on top. They are also good with cheese.

Ingredients

225g self-raising flour
½ level teaspoon salt (depending on taste)
150ml milk
10g butter

Makes 8

Method

Heat a flat-bottomed frying pan or griddle slowly to medium heat. Sieve flour, salt and baking powder into a baking bowl. Rub the butter into the dry ingredients and gradually add milk to create a light elastic dough. Use floured hands for the final mix. Divide dough into two. Roll out on a floured board into a round about 20mm thick. Cut into 4 triangles. Bake in a dry frying pan till just coloured, about 3-4 minutes each side. Cool on a cooling tray lightly wrapped in a clean tea-towel. Best eaten quite hot with lots of butter. Also good served with chunks of mature Cheddar cheese.

When cold, store any left-overs in a tin with a tight-fitting lid.

MISS LENNIE'S SCONES

Miss Lennie's potato scones
add a touch of reality
to a bizarre day.
          First
we have to flash down
the boiler men. They've
arrived unannounced four
days early. They can't find
our house, but today the village
seems crammed with lorries
all flashing lights in unison.

          No-one
speaks English. Communication
tests the limits of my partner's
Greek. Then we hear the cries
of a woman in distress.

          'They're out
to get me!' she shouts. 'Help me,
help me!' Tears pour down
her cheeks. I march her into
the kitchen, make a cup of tea,
place a KitKat in front of her.

          'Ron doesn't
love me any more,' she wails. 'He's
sent in men with guns.' I try my best
to reassure her, to calm her down.
My partner phones the husband
who's searching the village trying
in vain to find her.

We wait, he on jazz trumpet,
me trying out my long-forgotten
Samaritan skills in the kitchen.

          Eventually,
we reunite the demented woman
with her incredibly patient husband
Now an unexpected thunderstorm
and a downpour. We rush to
lower the sun umbrella.

          Frustration.
'I was going to bake potato
scones,' I say, gathering together
the pieces of our fragmented
morning.

          'So what's
keeping you?' my guy asks. I peel
potatoes, look out flour, salt,
a bit of butter, the frying pan.

          Ten minutes
later, we sit at the table tucking
into scones from Miss Lennie's
special recipe, scones hot from
the pan.
          A touch
of normality in a bizarre day.

POTATO SCONES

Not only a great way to use up leftover potatoes, but delicious in their own right. To be recommended.

Ingredients

225g cold mashed potatoes
15g butter
55g plain flour
½ level teaspoon salt
Pinch baking powder

Makes 8 scones

Method

Melt the butter and mix into the mashed potato (or if making from scratch mix the butter into the mashed potato then cool)

Divide the flour into 2. Mix the baking powder into the first half then, with your hand, work the flour into the potato. Mix the next half until you have a pliable dough. You might not need quite all the flour depending on the kind of potato.

Divide dough into two. Rollout each one thinly into a round. Cut into 4. Prick with a fork.

Bake on a hot griddle or flat frying pan for about 3 minutes each side.

Cool in a towel on a baking tray.

Eat with lots of butter.

TEA CEREMONY

I hear the doorbell, voices,
a few unfamiliar mumbled words.
    I slip
deeper into the hot suds, fragrant with expensive
toko-juzu, sip my drink. A knock, my husband
puts his head round the door, *A summons,* he says,
our new neighbours.
                73, you mean?
                  The very same.
          Now, this minute?
                  Wouldn't take no for an answer.
        You didn't tell them I'm in the bath?
                  My Japanese doesn't stretch that far.

I drain my gin-&-tonic, wrap myself in a towel,
go downstairs, stand by the window, watch
the deepening snow, relieved to be home from
a morning tutoring in the Brecon Beacons.
My husband checks his watch, *Better get a move on.*

    We dodge
across the road, bow, remove our shoes, follow
the couple into the living-room, bare of furniture,
except for a square table, barely ankle-height. We squat
on silk cushions, smile, make small-talk and the man translates.
Thigh muscles screaming, I get up, admire a set of dolls
displayed on red shelves.

Hina-Matsuri? I ask.
The woman beams with delight. *You know Hina-Matsuri?*
(I've used it in a book of festivals, so I'm on to a winner.)

Time for tea, the man says.
The couple disappear into the kitchen. My husband gets up
to stretch his legs, rubs his cold hands, *Saki?* he guesses.

A steaming silver kettle
and delicate tea-cups, black, bone-thin, are placed on the table.
We sit back down, wait. The woman brings in a giant-size jar
of Nescafe and four jam doughnuts. The man hands them round
with pride, *From Tesco, he says.*

TASTE OF HONEY

From the beginning

our dark was like
a hive of bees, murmurings,
the beating of wings.
We lay at the cross-roads
of night, dreams making
a bee-line for morning.

From the beginning

our joy was a talisman
against the backlash
of time. We tasted
honey on our lips, gossiped,
giggled, whispered, even
our silences were sweet.

From the beginning

we knew the end
was close, but veiled
the truth with *I love you's.*
And when it came, with
its sudden sunshine sting,
we were still candy-kissing.

AFTER THE HOTTEST DAY

Sometimes a ready meal
fills the bill, like tonight
sitting under a sun umbrella
in the cool of the evening
chores behind us –
pots watered,
filing, emails dealt with,
washing ironed, fresh
from the line, fruit in the fridge
ready for tomorrow's breakfast –
now it's wine-time
fountain burbling, Ottilie Patterson
singing *There'll be a hot time*
in the old town tonight, cold
white wine reaching my ankles,
an M&S microwave meal, raspberries
& cream, a scatter-brain breeze
troubling the trees. He takes
my hand, squeezes it, says
I'll bring things out, sets our meal
on the garden table. Geraniums
nod, share their true-blueness
their smattering of perfume.
He sings along to Ottilie's song,
I smile, content as a cat, listening,
I can't give you anything but love.